Animals must work hard to stay alive. Animals must watch out for predators. Predators are animals that eat other animals. Animals must find food. Food gives animals strength and energy.

   Animals must find shelter. Shelter keeps animals safe from people and other animals. Shelter also protects animals from all kinds of weather.

   Animals must do something if their habitat changes. A habitat is the area where an animal lives. If the habitat changes, then the animal might have to move to another place to live.

Zebras

Animals can stay safe by moving away from danger. Animals move away from danger by running, flying, or swimming.

Land animals run away from danger. A zebra can run away from a lion. A deer can run away from a black bear.

Animals with wings fly away to stay away from danger. A mosquito can fly away from a bullfrog. A robin can fly away from a cat.

Animals that live in the water swim away to avoid danger. A small fish can swim away from a larger fish.

HOW ANIMALS STAY ALIVE

by Richard P. Eggleston

SCHOOL PUBLISHERS

Cover, p.11, ©W. Perry Conway/CORBIS; p.3, ©Wolfgang Thieme/dpa/Corbis; p.4, ©Gallo Images/CORBIS; p.5, ©Joe McDonald/CORBIS; p.6, ©Vittoriano Rastelli/CORBIS; p.7, ©Corbis/PunchStock; p.8, ©Brandon D. Cole/CORBIS; p.9, ©Michael & Patricia Fogden/CORBIS; p.10, ©Cath Mullen; Frank Lane Picture Agency/CORBIS; p.12, ©Ron Sanford/CORBIS; p.13, ©Clive Druett; Papilio/CORBIS; p.14, ©Harcourt Telescope.

Copyright © by Harcourt, Inc.

All rights reserved. No part of this publication may be reproduced or transmitted in any form or by any means, electronic or mechanical, including photocopy, recording, or any information storage and retrieval system, without permission in writing from the publisher.

Requests for permission to make copies of any part of the work should be addressed to School Permissions and Copyrights, Harcourt, Inc., 6277 Sea Harbor Drive, Orlando, Florida 32887-6777. Fax: 407-345-2418.

HARCOURT and the Harcourt Logo are trademarks of Harcourt, Inc., registered in the United States of America and/or other jurisdictions.

Printed in China

ISBN 10: 0-15-350190-1
ISBN 13: 978-0-15-350190-6

Ordering Options
ISBN 10: 0-15-349939-7 (Grade 4 ELL Collection)
ISBN 13: 978-0-15-349939-5 (Grade 4 ELL Collection)
ISBN 10: 0-15-357281-7 (package of 5)
ISBN 13: 978-0-15-357281-4 (package of 5)

If you have received these materials as examination copies free of charge, Harcourt School Publishers retains title to the materials and they may not be resold. Resale of examination copies is strictly prohibited and is illegal.

Possession of this publication in print format does not entitle users to convert this publication, or any portion of it, into electronic format.

2 3 4 5 6 7 8 9 10 985 12 11 10 09 08 07

Toad

Some animals hide to escape danger. The bodies of these animals blend in with the area around them. This way of hiding is called camouflage. Some toads are brown. They live on the ground. Brown toads are hard to see if they are on brown ground.

Other animals act like they are dead to stay safe. If an opossum is in danger, it will lie on the ground and close its eyes. The opossum looks like it is dead. The predator leaves it alone.

Porcupine

Other animals stay safe because of their hard body parts. A porcupine has sharp quills, or spikes, on its back. When the porcupine sees danger, it sticks out its quills. The quills will injure a predator that tries to bite the porcupine.

An armadillo has hard plates on its body. The armadillo curls up into a ball when attacked. Most animals that attack the armadillo cannot bite through the hard plates.

Clams and snails have hard shells that protect them. Turtles have hard shells, too.

Mountain sheep

Some animals fight to stay safe. These animals usually have special body parts that help them fight. Mountain sheep have thick horns. The sheep ram into predators with these horns. Lions have sharp claws, and wild pigs have sharp tusks. Some snakes shoot poison into predators. Wasps and bees shoot poison, too.

Ostriches are large birds that have a sharp claw on one toe. Ostriches use this claw to cut predators. Skunks squirt a stinky liquid out of their bodies. This bad smell usually makes predators run away!

Baleen

All animals need food to stay alive. Most animals have special body parts that help them find and eat food. Some whales eat tiny sea creatures. These whales have baleen plates in their mouths. Baleen plates look like long strings. The plates hang from the top of the jaw to the bottom of the jaw. The whale opens its mouth and takes in water. The sea creatures get stuck in the plates. Then the whale eats the sea creatures.

Hummingbird

    Birds use their beaks to find and eat food. There are different kinds of beaks. Hawks and owls eat meat, so they have curved beaks. The curved beaks allow these birds to tear apart the meat. Hummingbirds eat nectar. Nectar is found in flowers. Hummingbirds have long, thin beaks so they can reach the nectar. Sparrows eat seeds. They have short beaks that they use to crack open the seeds.

All animals need shelter at times. Shelter is a safe place where animals can stay. Animals can protect themselves from humans, bad weather, and predators by finding shelter.

Many animals do not make homes. Instead, they move from place to place. These animals may find shelter only during very hot or cold weather.

Other animals build homes and live in them their whole lives. Some animals only build and live in homes when they are taking care of their young.

Beaver

Many animals do make homes. Raccoons and squirrels find shelter in hollow logs. Chipmunks are small animals like squirrels. Chipmunks build and live in burrows, which are holes in the ground. Owls may live inside of dead trees. Beavers build their homes in rivers or ponds. Beaver homes are made out of branches and mud. Bees make hives out of wax. Many bees live in these hives. Lions make dens for themselves. These dens may be in a cave or in a group of rocks.

Caribou

Animal habitats, or where animals live, can change for many reasons. Animals must do something when their habitat changes. Animals that do not do anything may not stay alive.

The weather in a habitat may change. The weather may become colder or hotter. Some animals go to another place when the weather changes.

Caribou are a type of deer that live in northern Canada. Caribou walk south to warmer weather before winter comes. They stay there until spring. Some whales swim to cooler waters in the summer. They may swim to warmer waters in the winter.

Some animals react to changes in their habitat by going into a deep sleep. This is called hibernating. Frogs hibernate when winter comes. Frogs dig a hole in the mud and stay there until spring. Some insects, such as bees, hibernate during the winter.

Many animals stay safe by living in groups. They live with other animals of their kind. Animals that live in groups help each other. For example, some animals in the group watch for danger. This lets other animals in the group eat or sleep.

Termites live in groups called colonies. Some birds live in groups called flocks. Some fish live in groups called schools. Together animals work hard to stay alive.

Scaffolded Language Development

COLLOCATIONS Point out the phrase *run away* in the sentence from the story, *Land animals run away from danger.* Explain to students that *run away* is a collocation, or a combination of words that occurs often. Review the collocations with the word *away* in the word bank. Have students choose the collocation that best completes each sentence. Then have students act out each sentence.

Word Bank: put away, flew away, gave away, ran away

1. A student _____ the books.
2. When the baby birds were old enough they _____ from their nest.
3. The host of the game show _____ a prize.
4. The elephant _____ from the mouse.

Science

Animal Dictionary Have students look back through the book and make a list of all the animal names they find. Then have them circle several of the animals on the list that they think go together and write a sentence to tell why they think they do.

School-Home Connection

More Examples Ask students to discuss this story with family members. Then have them think of other examples of animals staying safe, escaping danger, or finding food.

Word Count: 960 (968)